...Inc.

...ny form
...n storage
...embodied
...ng from its

Published by Sourcebooks, Inc.
P.O. Box 4410, Naperville, Illinois 60567–4410
(630) 961-3900
Fax: (630) 961-2168
www.sourcebooks.com

Printed and bound in China.
OGP 10 9 8 7 6 5 4 3 2 1

About the Illustrations and Font

Illustrators Charles Edmund Brock and his brother Henry Matthew Brock provided illustrations for many of the most popular books published on the cusp of the twentieth century. C. E. Brock completed illustrations for *Pride and Prejudice* in 1895, *Sense and Sensibility* in 1906, and various illustrations for *Emma*, *Northanger Abbey*, *Mansfield Park*, and *Persuasion* in 1907 and 1908. Both Charles and Henry illustrated for the six novels in the 1906 anthology *The Novels and Letters of Jane Austen* (Manor House Edition, edited by R. Brimley Jonnson). The two brothers shared a studio and were sources of great inspiration to one another.

The title font and where it appears internally throughout, aptly named "Jane Austen," is based on Austen's actual handwriting.

Introduction

On December 16, 1775, Jane Austen, one of the world's greatest novelists, was born. She was the seventh child born to Reverend George Austen and his wife, Cassandra. Having produced only six novels, she is nonetheless regarded as one of the most popular authors ever to come from England. Her novels, letters, and minor works have both touched the hearts of casual readers and exercised the brains of scholars. Jane is at the same time accessible and untouchable, and she has inspired a veritable industry of sequels, adaptations, movies, and miniseries.

On these pages you will find Jane's most honest and endearing thoughts on love. Let her advice guide you to finding happiness and contentment, just as the heroines in her novels always do.

Northanger Abbey

"He immediately rose"

MARRIAGE AND MATTERS
of the Heart

"To be so bent on marriage—to pursue a man merely for the sake of situation—is a sort of thing that shocks me; I cannot understand it. Poverty is a great evil, but to a woman of education and feeling it ought not, it cannot be the greatest. I would rather be a teacher at a school (and I can think of nothing worse) than marry a man I did not like."

—Emma in *The Watsons*

Pride and Prejudice

"And this offer of marriage you have refused?"

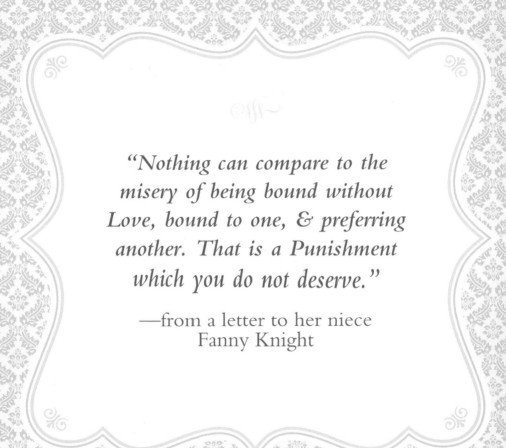

"*Nothing can compare to the misery of being bound without Love, bound to one, & preferring another. That is a Punishment which you do not deserve.*"

—from a letter to her niece
Fanny Knight

"Elinor perceived Willoughby"

"It is not time or opportunity that is to determine intimacy; it is disposition alone. Seven years would be insufficient to make some people acquainted with each other, and seven days are more than enough for others."

—Marianne Dashwood in
Sense and Sensibility

"He laughed most immoderately"

On Flirting

In the first surviving letter to her sister Cassandra, Jane reveals her flirtatious side: "I am almost afraid to tell you how my Irish friend and I behaved. Imagine to yourself everything most profligate and shocking in the way of dancing and sitting down together."

Pride and Prejudice

"Love and eloquence"

"It is a truth universally acknowledged, that a single man in possession of a good fortune must be in want of a wife."

—from *Pride and Prejudice*

"Most beloved Emma—tell me at once"

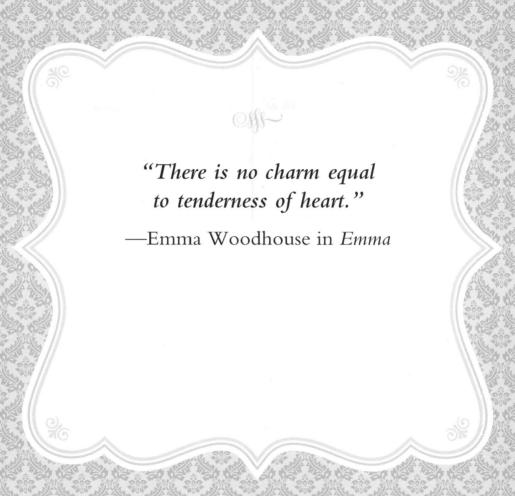

"*There is no charm equal to tenderness of heart.*"

—Emma Woodhouse in *Emma*

"With eyes of glowing entreaty fixed on her"

MARRIAGE AND MATTERS
of the Heart

"Anything is to be preferred or endured rather than marrying without Affection; and if his deficiencies of Manner &c &c strike you more than all his good qualities, if you continue to think strongly of them, give him up at once."

—from a letter to her niece Fanny Knight

"He then sat down by her"

"How little of permanent happiness could belong to a couple who were only brought together because their passions were stronger than their virtue."

—from *Pride and Prejudice*

"Sir Thomas brought him to her"

On Dancing

Dancing was very popular during Jane's time as it offered the perfect (and in some cases, the only) opportunity for flirtations and courtship. Jane loved to dance and referred to it often in letters to her sister:

"There were twenty dances, and I danced them all, and without any fatigue."

Sense and Sensibility

"The enjoyment of Elinor's company"

"A lady's imagination is very rapid; it jumps from admiration to love, from love to matrimony in a moment."

—Mr. Darcy in *Pride and Prejudice*

Mansfield Park

"*Miss Price all alone!*"

"A last and indubitable proof of Warren's indifference to me… he actually drew that gentleman's picture for me, and delivered it to me without a sigh."

—from a letter to her sister Cassandra

"I planned the match from that hour"

MARRIAGE AND MATTERS
of the Heart

"If a woman doubts as to whether she should accept a man or not, she certainly ought to refuse him. If she can hesitate as to 'Yes,' she ought to say 'No' directly. It is not a state to be safely entered into with doubtful feelings, with half a heart."

—Emma Woodhouse in *Emma*

"I was mad enough, however, to resent"

"The day is come on which I am to flirt my last with Tom Lefroy, and when you receive this it will be over. My tears flow as I write at the melancholy idea."

—from a letter to her sister Cassandra

"Standing together over the hearth"

On True Love

"I cannot fix on the hour, or the spot, or the look, or the words, which laid the foundation. It is too long ago. I was in the middle before I knew that I *had* begun."

—Mr. Darcy, after Elizabeth asks him when he began to fall in love with her, in *Pride and Prejudice*

"Just to leave a piece of paper on the table"

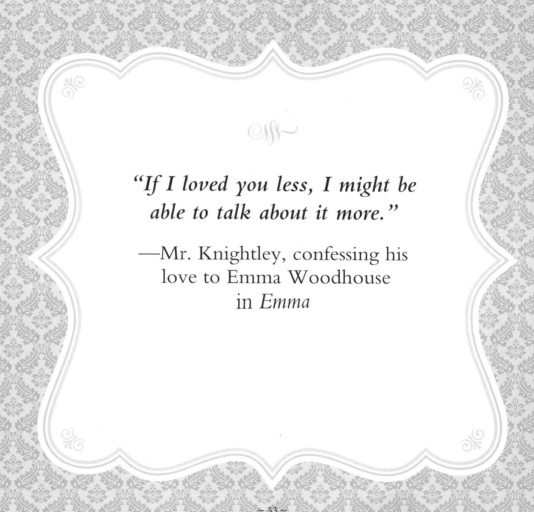

"If I loved you less, I might be able to talk about it more."

—Mr. Knightley, confessing his
love to Emma Woodhouse
in *Emma*

"*Of all the consequence in their power*"

"There are certainly not so many
men of large fortune in the world,
as there are pretty women
to deserve them."

—from *Mansfield Park*

"He… left them only at the door"

MARRIAGE AND MATTERS
of the Heart

"It is always incomprehensible to a man that a woman should ever refuse an offer of marriage."

—Emma Woodhouse in *Emma*

"Be so good as to look at his face"

"Friendship is certainly the finest balm for the pangs of disappointed love."

—from *Northanger Abbey*

"She was forced to listen"

On Optimism

"I pay very little regard...to what any young person says on the subject of marriage. If they profess a disinclination for it, I only set it down that they have not yet seen the right person."

—Mrs. Grant in *Mansfield Park*

"Drove her into a fainting fit"

"*Beware of swoons...Run
mad as often as you chuse* [sic]*;
but do not faint.*"

—Sophia in *Love and Friendship*

"Tell me, once and for all, are you engaged to him?"

"[Miss Bigg] writes me word that Miss Blackford is married, but I have never seen it in the papers, and one may as well be single if the wedding is not to be in print."

—from a letter to her sister
Cassandra

"He received the kindest welcome from her"

"*I suppose there may be a hundred different ways of being in love.*"

—Emma Woodhouse in *Emma*, on thinking Mr. Elton far too gallant

"I stood for a minute, feeling dreadfully"

On Love Lost

The writer of some of the greatest romances, Austen had very little personal experience to draw from. Aside from flirtation, her only brush with romantic love happened along a seashore with an unnamed man. When they parted, he made his intentions to meet with Jane again quite clear. However, news of his death reached her shortly after. No account of Jane's reaction to the news has been noted, though some believe this experience finds its way into *Persuasion*.

"You must allow me to present this young lady to you"

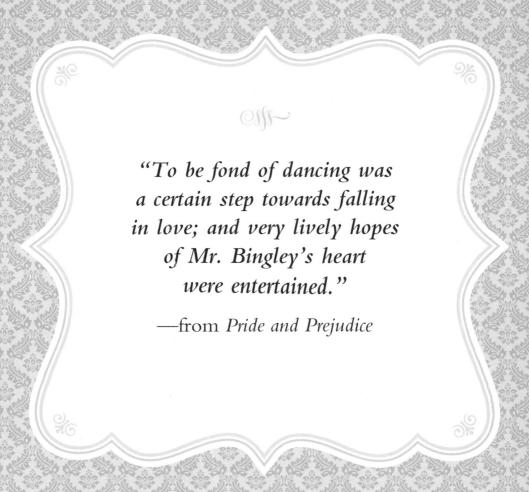

"To be fond of dancing was a certain step towards falling in love; and very lively hopes of Mr. Bingley's heart were entertained."

—from *Pride and Prejudice*

"Complete in his lieutenant's uniform"

MARRIAGE AND MATTERS
of the Heart

⚬⚬⚬

"I consider everybody as having a right to marry
once in their lives for love, if they can."

—from a letter to her sister Cassandra

Northanger Abbey

"*The General attended her himself to the street door*"

"She found his manners very pleasing indeed. The little flaw of having a Mistress now living with him at Ashdown Park, seems to be the only unpleasing circumstance about him."

—from a letter to her sister Cassandra

"Mr. Denny introduces his friend"

"When I consider how few young Men you have yet seen much of—how capable you are (yes, I do still think you very capable) of being really in love—and how full of temptation the next 6 or 7 years of your Life will probably be—(it is the very period of Life for the strongest attachments to be formed)—I cannot wish you with your present very cool feelings to devote yourself in honour to him."

—from a letter to her niece Fanny Knight

"It was at first a considerable shock to him"

MARRIAGE AND MATTERS
of the Heart

Jane Austen never married. However, Harris Bigg-Wither, a wealthy landowner, did propose on December 2, 1802. Austen accepted (though Bigg-Wither was a mere twenty-one to Austen's twenty-seven years). Following a sleepless night, Austen decided that she could not marry without love and withdrew her acceptance the next morning.

"Carried her down the hill"